VOYAGES OF DISCOVERY

Exploring the
World

Book Editor April McCroskie

Designed and produced by
The Salariya Book Company Ltd
Brighton, England.

Illustrated by Gerald Wood

Published by
PETER BEDRICK BOOKS
2112 Broadway
New York, NY 10023

Published in agreement with
Macdonald Young Books Ltd,
England

Library of Congress
Cataloging-in-Publication Data
Macdonald, Fiona.
  Exploring the world / Fiona
Macdonald, Gerald Wood.
    p.   cm. – (Voyages of discovery)
  Includes index.
  Summary: Tells the story of the first
explorers to travel around the world
and describes how and why these two
epic journeys came to be made.
  ISBN 0-87226-487-4
  1. Discoveries in geography –
Juvenile literature.
[1. Discoveries in geography.
2. Explorers.] I. Wood, Gerald.
II. Title. III. Series.
G175.M234 1996   96-1925
910'.9 – dc20   CIP
                                        AC

Printed in Hong Kong

00 99 98 97 96 1 2 3 4 5

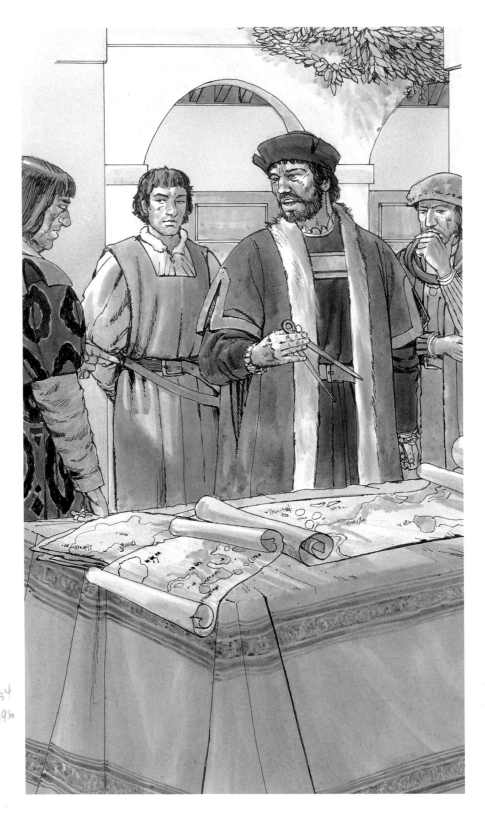

Exploring the World

Fiona Macdonald

Gerald Wood

PETER BEDRICK BOOKS

NEW YORK

CONTENTS

INTRODUCTION

This book tells the story of the first explorers to travel around the world:
the Spanish sea-captain Juan Sebastian del Cano, who completed a journey
planned and started by Portuguese nobleman Ferdinand Magellan, and the
English pirate and adventurer Sir Francis Drake. It also describes how and
why these two epic journeys – the first two "circumnavigations of the globe",
as they are often grandly titled – came to be made.

Over fifty years separate these two adventurous expeditions. Magellan set
sail in 1519, and Drake in 1577. One voyage barely covered its costs, the
other made a fortune for its backers. One expedition leader died tragically,
far from home. The other returned in triumph, as a hero. But in spite of these
differences, the first two voyages around the world both had an enormous
impact on politics, geographical knowledge and international trade.

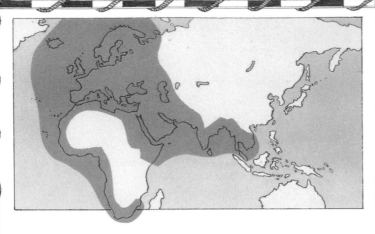

THIS MAP SHOWS the limits of the world known to European, North African and Asian explorers in the 15th century. North and South America, Australia, New Zealand and the Pacific islands were unknown.

Known lands

Early Explorers

How big is the earth? How many continents are there? What happens beyond the horizon? Is the earth round or flat? Questions like these puzzled explorers for thousands of years. To find answers, they made long journeys, took detailed measurements, worked out calculations and listened to travelers' tales. Religion played a part in exploration, too. Priests and scriptures from many faiths presented different pictures of the shape and size of the earth.

The first-known explorers – from ancient Egypt, Phoenicia and Greece – held several differing views. The Egyptians believed that the earth was a flat square, with pillars at each corner holding up the sky. The Greeks and Phoenicians also thought it was flat, but disk-shaped, and ringed by a boundless ocean. They knew of only three continents (because they had visited them): Europe, Asia and Africa. The rest of the earth was mysterious, risky and unknown.

But ideas were changing. Around 540 BC, the Greek mathematician Pythagoras suggested that the earth was round, like a ball. Then, around 350 BC, Aristotle, another Greek scholar, observed that the earth cast a curved shadow on the moon during an eclipse. This suggested that the earth had a curved surface.

In spite of these discoveries, the idea of a flat earth, limited to three continents, lasted for a very long time.

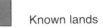

NORTH SEA

EUROPE

Carthage

AFRICA

ATLANTIC OCEAN

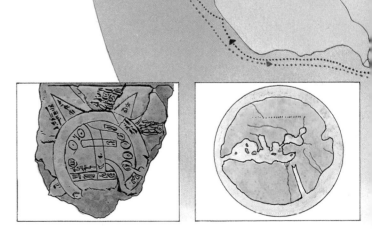

CARVED STONE MAP of the known world, made in Babylon around 600 BC. It shows dry land encircled by an ocean.

MAP based on the work of Greek geographer, Hecataeus, in the 5th century BC, showing lands around the Mediterranean Sea.

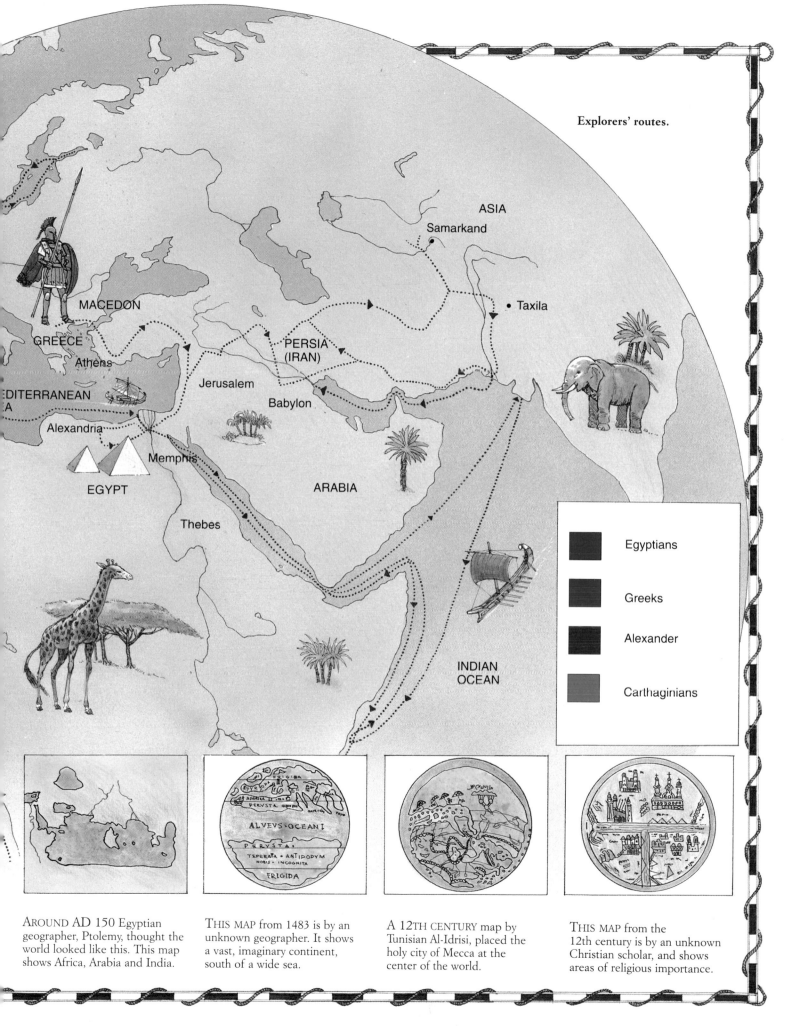

Explorers' routes.

ASIA

Samarkand

Taxila

MACEDON

GREECE

Athens

PERSIA
(IRAN)

MEDITERRANEAN
SEA

Jerusalem

Babylon

Alexandria

Memphis

EGYPT

Thebes

ARABIA

INDIAN
OCEAN

	Egyptians
	Greeks
	Alexander
	Carthaginians

AROUND AD 150 Egyptian geographer, Ptolemy, thought the world looked like this. This map shows Africa, Arabia and India.

THIS MAP from 1483 is by an unknown geographer. It shows a vast, imaginary continent, south of a wide sea.

A 12TH CENTURY map by Tunisian Al-Idrisi, placed the holy city of Mecca at the center of the world.

THIS MAP from the 12th century is by an unknown Christian scholar, and shows areas of religious importance.

7

Travelers' Tales

Conflicting ideas about the shape and size of the world were handed down from the ancient Greeks to Christian and Muslim scholars working in medieval times. But for many medieval people, common sense and everyday experience suggested that the world must be flat, whatever a few clever mathematicians and geographers might say. So, most medieval world maps continued to be drawn as flat-earth, three-continent designs. Many medieval maps were made to display religions rather than geographical ideas. Christian and Muslim scholars organized their pictures of the known world to show the holy cities of Jerusalem or Mecca at the center.

Medieval people were, however, prepared to believe that there might be parts of the world that explorers had not yet seen. Travelers' tales, written by daring adventurers, were very popular. They told stories of far-off cities, exotic peoples, terrible hardships, fabulous riches, enchanted forests, howling deserts and mountains that moved. Some tales were true and others were fantasies, but they were all very entertaining.

There were other travelers' tales that started as vague rumors, heard on the quayside in remote seaports. Had sailors from West Africa crossed the Atlantic to reach the Caribbean? Had Chinese travelers once visited the north coast of Australia? Were there really Viking settlers in America? Most medieval scholars never heard these sailors' "tall stories", but they were probably true.

EUROPEAN MERCHANT and traveler, Marco Polo, tasted fresh peppercorns in south-west India around AD 1280. Pepper and other spices were rare and valuable in medieval Europe. Explorers made long, dangerous journeys to bring back spices, silks and perfumes from the East. They sold them at high prices and made huge profits.

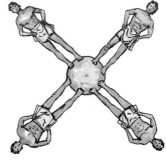

SOME MEDIEVAL SCHOLARS thought that if the world were round, half the people on it would have to walk about upside down.

MAP OF THE WORLD in 1448, drawn by German monk Andreus Walsperger. He has drawn North at the bottom, and the holy city of Jerusalem at the center.

TRAVELERS half-expected to meet monsters in distant lands. Marco Polo traveled in the East between 1271 and 1295. He reported seeing men with faces in their chests, dog-headed men and men with one foot big enough to be used as a sunshade.

GEOGRAPHERS in their studies and sailors far out at sea used scientific instruments like astrolabes and armillary spheres to help them observe the movements of stars and planets.

A geographer studies an astrolabe.

THIS ILLUSTRATION, from a textbook written in 1519, shows the goddess of astronomy and the famous geographer, Ptolemy, giving advice to a student of geography.

9

Sailing to America

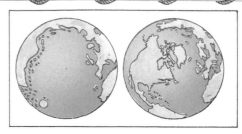

By the late 15th century, many scholars were prepared to accept that the world was round. But their knowledge was entirely theoretical. How could it be proved?

The first great discovery was made by an unlikely person: a wool-worker's son from Genoa, called Christopher Columbus. Like most explorers, Columbus dared to take amazing risks because he was ambitious. He wanted money, knowledge and power, and had worked out a way to make his fortune. Columbus believed he could find a sea-route to the rich lands of the East by traveling westwards across the Atlantic Ocean.

In 1492, Columbus set sail westwards from southern Spain into the unknown. Many people who watched him leave felt sure they would never see him again. What if the old maps were right? What if the world was flat? What if Columbus and his ships were swallowed up in the vast, encircling ocean?

They need not have worried. Columbus reached land (the Bahama Islands) safely, and returned to tell the tale. Columbus died believing he had sailed to Japan. But many scholars realized that he had discovered something even more important than a sea-route to the East. He had found a whole new continent, which they called America. The old maps of the world would have to be re-drawn. But how? What other lands lay beyond the horizon, further round the world?

LEFT: the world as Columbus imagined, with sea between Europe and Asia.
RIGHT: the world as it really is, with America in between.

ILLUSTRATIONS from a book published in 1493. They show (*left to right*) the Atlantic Ocean with the King of Spain on one side and Caribbean people running away from Columbus's ships on the other; an imaginary European-style town in the Caribbean; local people behind trees, watching Columbus arrive.

THE ROUTE FOLLOWED by Columbus to make his first Atlantic crossing, in 1492. His voyage took 61 days. From 1493-1504, Columbus made three more voyages to America. He died in 1506, still believing he had reached the East.

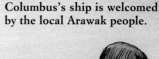

First voyage 1492-3

Second voyage 1493-4

Fourth voyage 1502-4

Columbus's ship is welcomed by the local Arawak people.

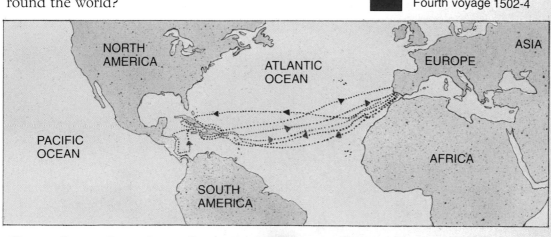

NORTH AMERICA

ATLANTIC OCEAN

EUROPE

ASIA

PACIFIC OCEAN

AFRICA

SOUTH AMERICA

WHEN COLUMBUS anchored off the Bahamas, the local Arawak people came out to welcome him. They gave gifts of parrots, spears tipped with fish-teeth and cotton thread. Columbus gave them glass beads, red caps and metal bells.

COLUMBUS and his crew crossed the Atlantic in three sailing ships: *(left to right) Santa Maria, Pinta* and *Niña*. Their journey was dangerous but exciting. In his journal, Columbus wrote, "It is important that I forget sleep and labor much at navigation."

Round Africa to the East

PRINCE HENRY THE NAVIGATOR of Portugal (1394-1460), paid for many voyages by Portuguese explorers, who sailed along the west coast of Africa and out to the Azores.

At the same time as Columbus was making plans to sail west, Portuguese explorers were looking for another new sea-route to the East. They aimed to sail eastwards round the southernmost tip of Africa, which they optimistically named the "Cape of Good Hope".

Since 1418, Portuguese sailors had been surveying the west coast of Africa, encouraged by Prince Henry of Portugal. His enthusiasm for exploration was so great that he was nicknamed "Henry the Navigator", although he never made a long voyage out to sea.

Until the Portuguese explorations started, Europeans knew nothing about Africa south of the Sahara. Arab and other Muslim merchants, and a few Chinese travelers, were familiar with east-African coastal lands. But European explorers did not know much about these expeditions. Some European geographers believed there could be no sea-route around Africa. Any ship traveling so far south would be swept away for ever in mountainous seas. A few scholars predicted gloomily that sailors venturing into tropical heat would be baked alive by the sun.

Henry the Navigator died in 1460, but Portuguese exploration continued. From 1487-8, Bartolomeu Dias sailed round the Cape of Good Hope and into the Indian Ocean. In 1498 Vasco da Gama reached India by the same route. Once again, the map-makers were busy, as more and more was being discovered about the shape and size of the world.

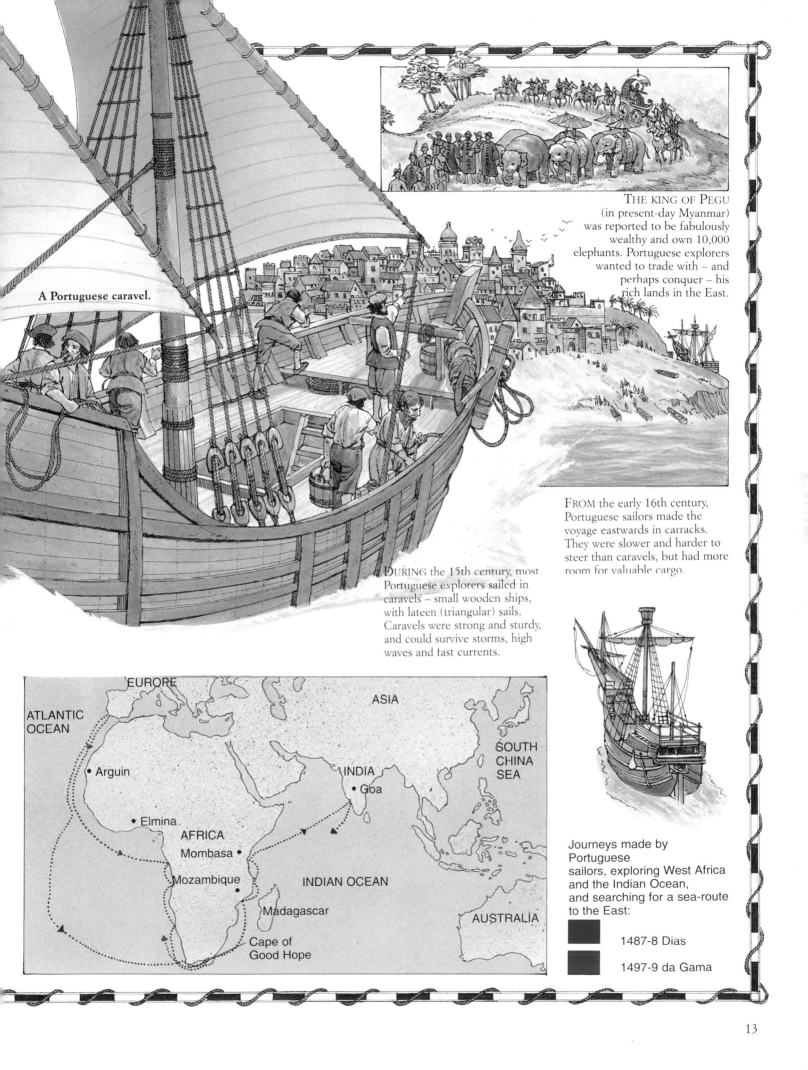

A Portuguese caravel.

THE KING OF PEGU (in present-day Myanmar) was reported to be fabulously wealthy and own 10,000 elephants. Portuguese explorers wanted to trade with – and perhaps conquer – his rich lands in the East.

FROM the early 16th century, Portuguese sailors made the voyage eastwards in carracks. They were slower and harder to steer than caravels, but had more room for valuable cargo.

DURING the 15th century, most Portuguese explorers sailed in caravels – small wooden ships, with lateen (triangular) sails. Caravels were strong and sturdy, and could survive storms, high waves and fast currents.

EUROPE

ASIA

ATLANTIC OCEAN

• Arguin

INDIA
• Goa

SOUTH CHINA SEA

• Elmina

AFRICA

Mombasa •

Mozambique •

INDIAN OCEAN

Madagascar

AUSTRALIA

Cape of Good Hope

Journeys made by Portuguese sailors, exploring West Africa and the Indian Ocean, and searching for a sea-route to the East:

1487-8 Dias

1497-9 da Gama

Ships and Sailors

The *Vittoria*, sailed by Ferdinand Magellan, and the *Golden Hind*, sailed by Francis Drake, were the first ships to travel around the world.
To modern eyes, they would look astonishingly small. Drake's *Golden Hind* was around 100 feet long and 20 feet wide, and could carry about 100 tons. The *Vittoria* was smaller, carrying only 85 tons.

Both ships were old and had many repairs. Yet they withstood salt-water, tropical heat, fierce gusts of wind and rain, rats, mice, wood-boring worms and waves 30 feet high.

The sailors were rough, wild and, mostly, unwilling. Few men were keen to sign on for a voyage that was likely to end in death. Magellan's sailors came from all over Europe – he took anyone he could find. Drake tricked his crew by saying they were going to Africa. They were not pleased when they found out they were sailing around the world.

VITTORIA, the first-ever ship to sail around the world (1519-21).

GOLDEN HIND, the second ship to sail around the world (1577-80).

Deck

A SAILING SHIP was built round a massive timber "backbone", called a keel. Curved wooden ribs were added, to make a framework for the hull. Wooden planks were softened with steam so they could bend and were then nailed to the ribs.

Wooden planks

Both the *Vittoria* and the *Golden Hind* also had gentlemen-adventurers on board; friends of rich people who had invested money in the voyage. They hoped to make their fortunes and to escape from boredom at home. But they were a nuisance. They did not know how to sail a ship, and they refused to obey orders. Magellan and Drake both faced mutinies; Magellan hanged some trouble-makers and abandoned the others on shore. Drake held a show trial and beheaded one of his men as a warning to his rebellious crew. Afterwards, everyone behaved.

Ribs

OAK was the best – and most expensive – timber to use for shipbuilding. It was sawn by hand, and trimmed to shape with a tool called an adze. Gaps between planks were packed with hemp-fiber then coated with tar to make the hull waterproof.

Caulking (hemp fiber) between planks

Building a sailing ship.

Keel

15

SAILORS USED a traverse board – marked like a compass and drilled with holes – to record a ship's course. Every 30 minutes, a peg was put into one of the holes to show the direction steered.

A CROSS-STAFF helped sailors work out latitude by measuring the angle of the sun above the horizon at noon, or the Pole Star at night. Both appeared lower in the sky the further away a ship was from the equator.

THE CROSS-STAFF was fitted with sliding cross-pieces, called transoms, used to help measure the angle of the sun.

Transom

Cross-staff

Compass

Traverse board

Kemal

THE ARAB KEMAL (a square of animal horn attached to a knotted rope) could also be used to measure the angle of the sun above the horizon.

Navigation

Sailors navigating a ship in familiar seas knew where to look out for dangerous rocks or treacherous shallows. They needed only simple things to help them navigate: local landmarks (to work out their position), lead-lines (to measure the depth of the water and examine the condition of the sea bed) and log-lines (to measure their ship's speed).

But sailors exploring unknown seas and oceans needed much more elaborate equipment for navigating, especially if there was no land in sight and they were sailing across oceans thousands of feet deep. Landmarks and lead-lines were no use to them there. On unknown oceans there was danger, too, from unpredictable weather conditions.

Explorers always needed to know their exact position at sea. Only then could they work out the best course to steer towards their next landfall. If they got lost, they might never find land and would die from thirst and starvation.

Different instruments for navigation.

SPEED was measured by a log-line – a kind of knotted rope – dropped into the sea. The faster it unwound from its reel, the faster the ship was going. The sea's depth was measured by lead-lines – heavy weights tied to ropes and lowered overboard. Some leads had hollow bases to collect samples from the sea bed.

Lead-line

Log-line

AN ASTROLABE was a metal disk with moveable "pointers" used to measure latitude. It was accurate, but metal was expensive.

Astrolabe

AN ARMILLARY SPHERE was a model showing stars and planets in the skies above the earth. It helped sailors work out their position at sea, by observing which stars were overhead.

Armillary sphere

16TH-CENTURY COMPASS. The needle pointed to magnetic north and helped explorers to steer. A sand-glass (*below*) measured time. It took 30 minutes for sand to fall between chambers.

Sand-glass

Explorers setting off across uncharted seas – like Columbus and Magellan – did not know where they were going, or whether they would ever find land. They were extraordinarily brave. Fifteenth and sixteenth-century navigators measured their position at sea in degrees of latitude; that is, how far they were north or south of the equator. To do this they used an instrument called a cross-staff, a kemal or an astrolabe. They also kept a rough record of how they had steered, using a traverse board and a written account of their voyage in the ship's journal, or "log".

BEFORE DETAILED MAPS and charts were made, many explorers' ships were wrecked in uncharted seas.

Two Great Explorers

The map on this page shows the routes taken by the two greatest sailors of the sixteenth century – Ferdinand Magellan and Francis Drake. Both explorers followed approximately the same route. Both were intelligent, brave and determined. But in almost everything else they were very different.

Magellan was a nobleman and a full-time soldier. His character was formal, dignified and stern, but straightforward, honest and honorable. He had spent many years in the East and knew India and the Spice Islands well, but he was not an experienced navigator. After Columbus had discovered America, it was Magellan's idea to look for a sea-route around the south of the "new-found" continent.

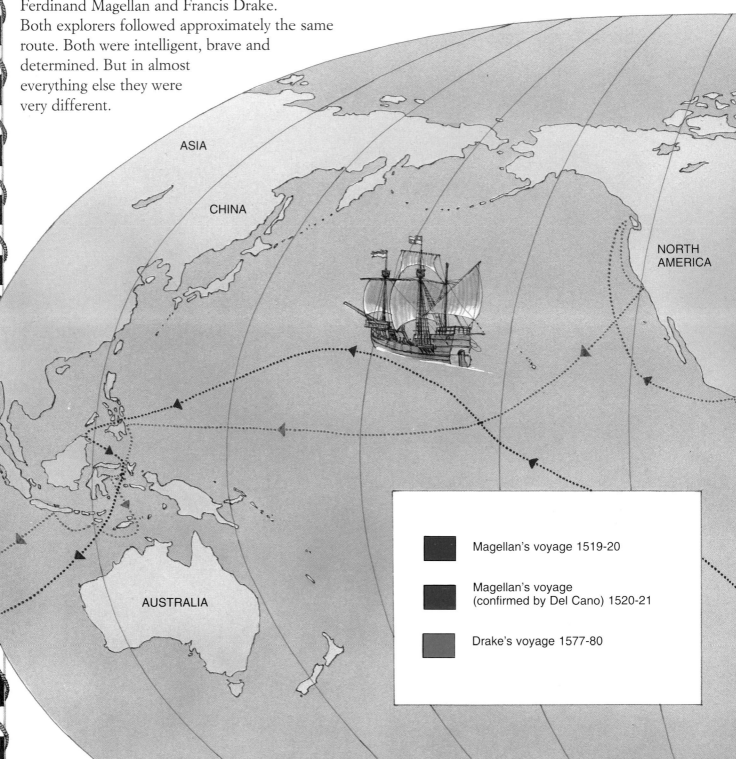

ASIA

CHINA

NORTH AMERICA

AUSTRALIA

■	Magellan's voyage 1519-20
■	Magellan's voyage (confirmed by Del Cano) 1520-21
■	Drake's voyage 1577-80

Tragically, Magellan died far from home, and the sailors who continued his voyage won the praise and fame that rightly belonged to him.

Drake's family was not noble. He was brought up on a hulk – an old, rotting ship used as a houseboat. But even as a very young man, it was obvious that he had exceptional seafaring skills. He was enthusiastic, hot-tempered and a great leader.

He was deeply patriotic and hated Spain. People either loved him or hated him, but most people he met – from Queen Elizabeth to ordinary sailors – seemed to fall under his spell. He was able to build on other people's achievements and turn them to his own advantage – especially if they were likely to make him rich.

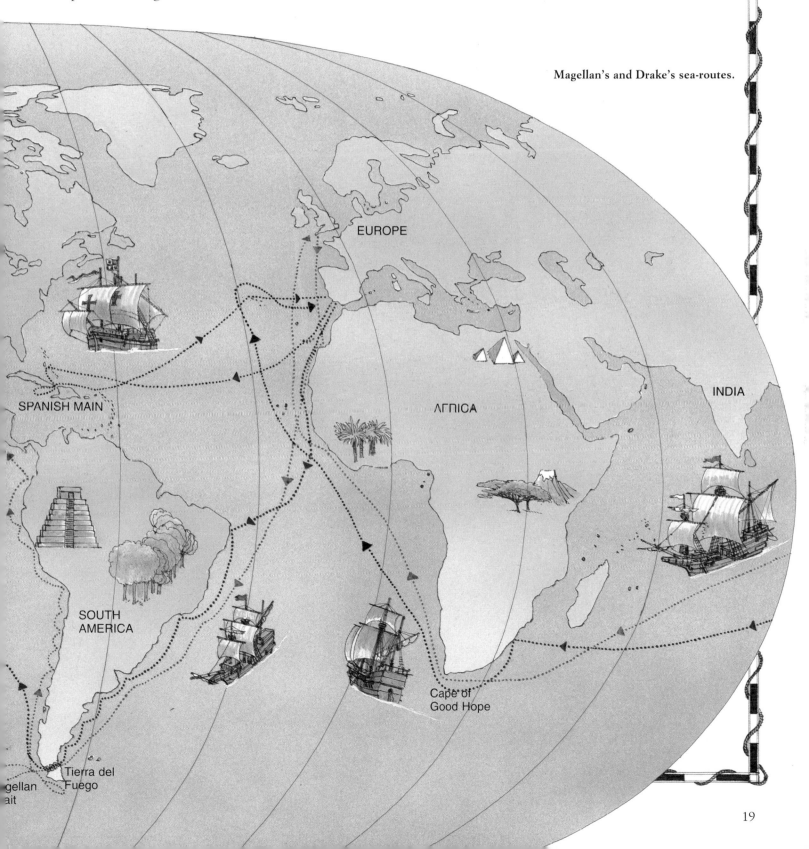

Magellan's and Drake's sea-routes.

EUROPE

SPANISH MAIN

AFRICA

INDIA

SOUTH AMERICA

Cape of Good Hope

Tierra del Fuego

gellan ait

Magellan sets sail

In 1517, Ferdinand Magellan requested a meeting with King Charles of Spain. He took with him a model globe and a bold new idea. This was to ask King Charles to sponsor a great adventure he was planning: to explore the oceans around South America, in the hope of finding a westward sea-route to the Spice Islands of the East.

Magellan also told King Charles he was sure he could prove that the rich Spice Islands (part of present-day Indonesia) lay within Spain's share of the "New World". (All the newly-discovered lands of America and the Far East had been shared between Spain and Portugal by the Treaty of Tordesillas in 1494).

Magellan was Portuguese, and had spent many years fighting for his country. So why was he meeting the king of Spain, Portugal's neighbor and traditional enemy? We do not know for certain, but there were rumors at the time that Magellan had quarreled with the Portuguese king, Manuel. Whatever the reason, King Charles of Spain did not care. He thought Magellan's scheme was a good one and agreed to help. By August 1519, Magellan and his five ships were ready to sail from Seville. They left dreaming of great discoveries. But sadly, Magellan never saw Spain or Portugal again. Among his ships, only the little *Vittoria* survived.

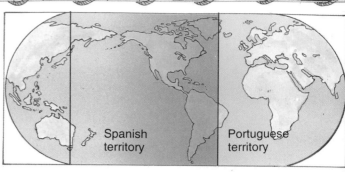

Spanish territory

Portuguese territory

IN 1494, Spain and Portugal signed an agreement, called the Treaty of Tordesillas, about who should rule lands claimed by their explorers in America and the Far East.

UNKNOWN TO MAGELLAN, his ships were loaded with rotten food, in the hope of sabotaging the voyage. Spanish spies were also "planted" among Magellan's crew. Magellan's family and friends suspected this was organized by King Manuel of Portugal, after Magellan's quarrel with him.

Magellan's ship being loaded in Seville, Spain.

PORTUGUESE SHIPS sailed eastwards to India through wild, stormy seas off the Cape of Good Hope at the southern tip of Africa. Magellan wanted to find a better route.

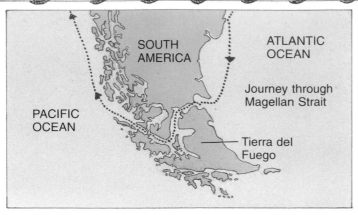

SOUTH
AMERICA

ATLANTIC
OCEAN

Journey through
Magellan Strait

PACIFIC
OCEAN

Tierra del
Fuego

MAGELLAN did not follow
Columbus's route across the
Atlantic. To avoid being chased
by Portuguese ships, he sailed
southwards towards Africa,
then west until he reached Brazil.

BY MARCH 1520, Magellan's
ships had reached Patagonia.
Magellan and his crew were the
first Europeans to see the wild
landscape at the southernmost
tip of America.

Across the Atlantic

Magellan finally set sail in August 1519. It was not an impressive start. He had five battered, second-hand ships and a crew of 237 men recruited from the most disreputable dockside taverns in Europe. Only a few officers, like Juan Sebastian del Cano from the Basque country in northern Spain, were experienced navigators. Magellan relied on them to give him good advice.

It was almost three months before they managed to sight land. Magellan's ships got caught in the doldrums, where the winds rarely blow and where it is stiflingly hot. The crew had never sailed this far before, so they were anxious and miserable.

By Christmas 1519, they were off the coast of southern Brazil. Magellan sent a boat ashore for luscious tropical fruit, to give the crew a treat. This brought peace on board for a while, but by March 1520, the crew were mutinous. Magellan decided on firm action, and executed the leaders. He wanted to hang del Cano along with the other rebels, but could not do without his seafaring skills.

As they sailed further south, the weather became cold, wet and very stormy. One ship, the *Santiago*, was wrecked, and the others were thrown around by violent gales. The sailors had never seen such terrible weather, and feared they would be drowned. But Magellan insisted on exploring further south. In October, his persistence was rewarded; he found the entrance to a channel which led round the tip of South America to the vast Pacific Ocean.

The weather is very stormy off the southern tip of South America.

IN OCTOBER 1520, after months of exploring, Magellan and his crew found the entrance to the channel leading from the Atlantic to the Pacific, now called the Magellan Strait. It is about 320 miles long and took Magellan's ships 35 days to sail.

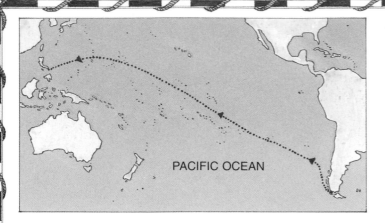

MAGELLAN'S SHIPS sailed across the Pacific for 3 months and 20 days without passing any land. On January 24,1521 they sighted islands, but the water was too deep to anchor.

ON BOARD SHIP, the crew ran out of fresh food and water. They ate whatever they could find, including sawdust, insects and old leather. Mice were sold for half a gold coin each.

Into the Pacific

Magellan's ships entered the Pacific Ocean on November 28,1520. He and his crew were the first Europeans ever to sail on the world's largest ocean, but a terrible ordeal lay ahead. It was almost four months before they next came ashore.
From Magellan's earlier travels in the east, he knew the approximate latitude (position north of the equator) of the Spice Islands. But he had no real idea of how far the distance between them and the west coast of South America might be.

Magellan first caught sight of land at the end of January 1521. There was nowhere for his ships to anchor, so he had to pass by. Understandably, he named it "Disappointment Isle" (probably near the present-day Marquesas Islands). In March 1521, Magellan finally found safe anchorage at a group of Pacific islands he named "the Philippines".

The local chief was friendly. He offered fresh food and water, and a sheltered beach where Magellan could repair his ships. After talking to Magellan (who was deeply religious) the chief and 800 of his people decided to become Christians. They asked also for Magellan's help in fighting a local war. Magellan and his crew agreed. They thought that their crossbows and guns would easily defeat the local soldiers, armed only with spears. But they were outnumbered and quickly overpowered. Magellan and 40 of his men were killed on the beach, as they tried to escape. The rest were now without a leader nearly 8,000 miles from home.

Magellan and his men are killed.

MOST SAILORS got a disease called scurvy. Their gums bled, their joints ached and they got sores. Magellan stayed fit as he had a private supply of quince marmalade full of vitamin C.

ON MARCH 6, 1520, they reached safe anchorage at last, at the remote island of Guam. They bought rice, fresh fruit and water, but left quickly, claiming the islanders were thieves.

ON MARCH 16, Magellan's ships anchored at a group of islands. Magellan called them "the Philippines", in honor of Prince Philip, son of the King of Spain who financed his voyage.

MAGELLAN and his crew received gifts from the local chief: fish, bananas, palm oil and coconuts. In return, Magellan gave bells, mirrors and lengths of colored cloth.

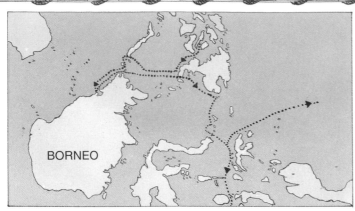

BORNEO

Del Cano

The *Trinidad*

THE TEREDO WORM bores holes in ships' timbers, making them crumble. By 1521, it had destroyed the ship *Concepcion*. Now only two of Magellan's fleet of five ships remained.

LED BY DEL CANO, Magellan's crew set sail for the Spice Islands in June 1521. On the way, they behaved like pirates, robbing local vessels and capturing local sailors who would help them sail their ships.

The Spice Islands

By April 1521, only 115 of Magellan's crew were alive, and only two of his five ships remained seaworthy. Now that Magellan was dead, the Portuguese nobleman Carvalho took command. He and his crew decided to cruise around the Philippines for two months' piracy, trying to get rich. In June, they set sail for the Spice Islands, robbing local people and capturing local sailors, whom they forced to show them the way. By November, they reached the Spice Islands, laden with loot.

Although the sultan was suspicious, he allowed them to trade. But their good fortune did not last – Carvalho and many others died from fevers. One ship – the *Trinidad* was rotten. As soon as they filled it with cargo, it began to leak.

Juan Sebastian del Cano was the senior surviving captain. In December 1521, he decided to head back to Europe, sailing westwards across the Indian Ocean in the little ship *Vittoria*. It had 47 survivors from Magellan's original crew, plus 13 local sailors.

The larger *Trinidad* stayed in harbor to be mended. Later, loaded with 50 tons of precious cloves, it set off eastwards back across the Pacific, heading for Europe via the Magellan Strait. But disaster struck. The *Trinidad* met constant contrary winds, and 30 men out of its crew of 53 got scurvy and died. The *Trinidad* sailed back to the Spice Islands, where it was captured by the Portuguese. Its crew were put in prison, and many of them died. Only four ever got back to Spain.

TREASURES from the Spice Islands: 1 Ginger 2 Cassia 3 Cloves 4 Cinnamon 5 Pepper 6 Nutmeg. Magellan's crew hoped also to find precious silks, pearls, parrots and sandalwood to take home to Europe.

Trading goods on shore.

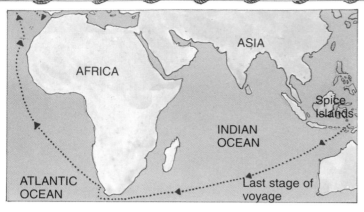

Table top mountain at
Cape of Good Hope

The Long Voyage Home

It had taken Magellan's crew 27 months to sail to the Spice Islands. The voyage home was shorter, but still dangerous and very long. The *Vittoria* set sail, still heading west, in December 1521. Europeans had traveled this way before, but the seas were still hazardous and largely unknown. They were also claimed by Portugal as part of its overseas empire. The *Vittoria* was Spanish, and paid for by the Spanish king. Its crew were weak – though determined – and an easy target for any well-armed Portuguese.

In March 1522, del Cano and his crew sighted the east-African coast. They did not dare to land, even though they were, once again, short of food and water. They did not want to meet Portuguese shipping there, so they headed south, around the Cape of Good Hope. They lost their way and were blown far south, to dangerous currents, violent winds and mountainous waves. The little *Vittoria* was badly damaged, and almost sank.

Finally, they managed to head northwards, and rounded the Cape. In June, they crossed the equator, but by now they were all very ill. In July, in desperation, they went ashore at the Cape Verde islands, even though these belonged to the Portuguese. The risk of a fight seemed better than starvation at sea. They exchanged some of their spices for fresh fruit and rice – then had to run for their lives when Portuguese soldiers arrived on the beach. Thirteen of the crew were captured and taken off to prison.

EARLY IN MAY 1522, Magellan's crew rounded the Cape of Good Hope. They were now back in fairly well-known waters. But the crew were ill with scurvy, the ship was falling apart and food was running short.

The desperate crew sight land at last.

IN FEBRUARY 1522, Magellan's crew left Madagascar and set sail for the east-African coast. They sailed past prosperous trading towns and well-defended forts, but they did not dare to land for fear of being attacked. By now they had been away from Spain for over two years and were desperate to get home.

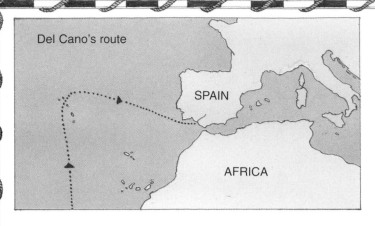
Del Cano's route

SPAIN

AFRICA

Back in Spain

On September 8, 1522, del Cano steered the sea-stained, tattered *Vittoria* up the River Guadalquivir to the port of Seville. Out of Magellan's original crew, there were only 18 Europeans, who had joined the ship in the Far East, and four Spice Islanders. The local people were shocked and surprised to see Magellan's ship return, but del Cano and the survivors were given a tremendous welcome and honored as heroes. Even the Portuguese, who were long-time enemies of Spain, released the 13 sailors they had imprisoned on the Cape Verde Islands, and sent them back to Spain to join the rest of the survivors from the first-ever voyage around the world.

Everyone wanted to hear all about the crew's adventures. Here was a traveler's tale to beat any that had been told before. Even King Charles summoned them to meet him at his royal palace nearby; he wanted to hear what "his" expedition to the Spice Islands had achieved. He also wanted to know whether it had made a profit. This was, after all, Magellan's original aim when he had first suggested the voyage.

Sadly, there was no profit to give to King Charles. The *Vittoria* arrived at Seville with 25 tons of cloves on board. When they were sold, they made just enough money to cover the original cost, over three years ago, of fitting out Magellan's five ships, and of paying and feeding his original crew. There was nothing left over at the end.

The Vittoria docks in Seville.

On September 9, 1522, the day after they arrived home, the surviving sailors from Magellan's expedition took part in a barefoot procession through the streets, carrying lighted candles, to the church of Santa Maria de la Vittoria in Seville. There, they said prayers to give thanks. They knew they had been extraordinarily fortunate: out of Magellan's original crew of 237, only they had returned.

The people of Seville could hardly believe their eyes when, nearly three years after it had set off to sail around the world, Magellan's ship Vittoria sailed into port. Everyone thought it had been lost long ago.

A New View of the World

From a short-term point of view, the first voyage around the world had been a disaster. Its ships had been lost, its commander and almost all the sailors on board had died, and it had failed to make a profit. Magellan's reputation was ruined: del Cano blamed him, very unfairly, for all that had gone wrong with the expedition.

To make matters worse, the kings of Spain and Portugal were still arguing over who had the exclusive right to trade with the Spice Islands. (This dispute finally ended in 1527, when King Charles sold all of Spain's rights in the Spice Islands to Portugal for 350,000 golden ducats. He did this because he was running short of money to pay for a war with France).

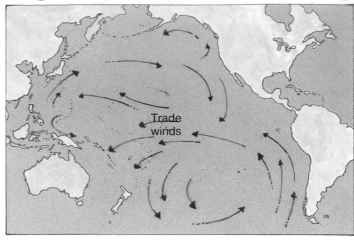

Trade winds

GEOGRAPHERS, map-makers and navigators were keen to find out more about Magellan and del Cano's voyage. Antonio Pigafetta, a sailor on Magellan's ship, wrote a book about the journey.

PIGAFETTA'S FRONT-COVER drawing (*above*) shows islands in the Pacific Ocean, and a Pacific outrigger canoe.

FOR MOST OF THE YEAR, "trade winds" blow in one direction – from America to Asia – across the Pacific Ocean. They helped Magellan's ships reach the Philippines, by blowing behind them and speeding them on their way.

But the same trade winds made it very difficult and dangerous for ships trying to sail in the opposite direction. They had to spend months at sea, far out of sight of land, battling against strong winds and rough seas. Even if they avoided being wrecked, few sailing ships had enough space on board for food and water to last for such a long voyage.

These difficulties meant that every voyage to the Spice Islands by Magellan's westwards route would have to be a circumnavigation – still a frightening prospect for even the most adventurous sailors in the early 16th century.

MAGELLAN AND DEL CANO'S voyage had proved beyond doubt that the world was round and not flat. Geographers from the 16th century made globes like this, to display their new-found knowledge.

AFTER the *Vittoria* returned from its epic voyage, world maps had to be revised. This 16th-century map (*right*), drawn by Battista Agnese, shows Magellan and del Cano's route. It shows the Magellan Strait and the Pacific Ocean quite accurately, but leaves out Australia and many Pacific islands. European explorers did not yet know about them.

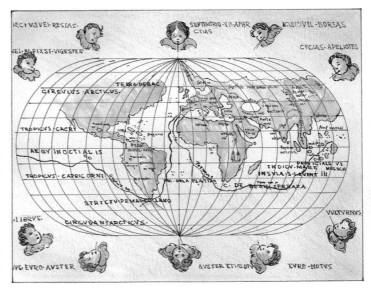

Even del Cano's fame and fortune did not last long. He died in the Pacific in 1525, trying to make the second circumnavigation of the globe. However, from a long-term point of view, Magellan, del Cano and their crew had achieved a tremendous success. They had established, beyond doubt, that the world was round and not flat. They had also proved that it was possible for a ship to sail right around the globe, without falling off the edge, being tipped upside down, or getting swept away by an encircling ocean. They had found the best route for ships to use when sailing across the Pacific – although at the same time, they discovered that the Portuguese eastward route to the Spice Islands was shorter and safer.

BACK HOME in Spain, del Cano became a hero. He bought a new house, lots of fine new clothes and befriended two beautiful mistresses. He planned many new adventures with nobles and navigators, all eager to make their fortunes in the rich Spice Islands.

Planning new expeditions.

Pirate

Spanish sailors attack Drake and Hawkins at San Juan d'Ulloa on the Mexican coast

IN AUGUST 1568, Drake and Hawkins looked for shelter in the Spanish port of San Juan d'Ulloa, after their ship was damaged in a storm. At first, the Spaniards were friendly.

Francis Drake grew up on an old rotting houseboat moored on the River Thames in London. Around 1555, when he was about 12 years old, Drake was apprenticed to the owner of a small cargo ship that ferried goods between England, the Low Countries and France. When the owner died, around 1560, Drake ran the ferry business for several years. But he was bored and dreamed of new horizons and the possibility of making lots of money. When pirate and slave-trader John Hawkins asked Drake to join his crew on a voyage to Africa and the Caribbean, Drake jumped at the chance.

Hawkins was a very experienced seaman and navigator, so he taught Drake how to handle a ship in tropical seas. Drake and Hawkins shared many adventures. Some were brave and patriotic, like their attacks on the foreign sailors who threatened English merchant ships. Others, like their slave-raids in Africa, were bloodthirsty and cruel. After they were attacked by Spanish sailors at San Juan d'Ulloa, Drake developed a lifelong hatred of Spain. In 1572, he left Hawkins' crew, and started to make voyages to the Caribbean as a raider and pirate on his own.

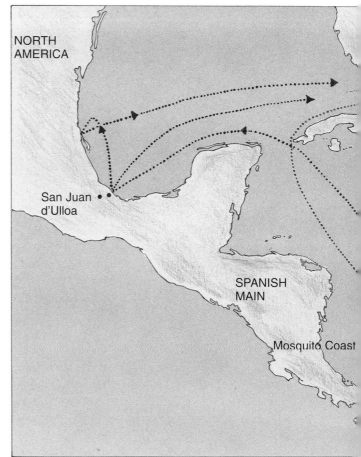

NORTH AMERICA

San Juan d'Ulloa

SPANISH MAIN

Mosquito Coast

THEN SPANISH SHIPS arrived with high-ranking officers on board. They gave orders to attack the English. Many men were massacred; Drake and Hawkins were lucky to escape.

ENGLISH AND SPANISH RIVALRIES

There were many reasons for rivalry. Spain was staunchly Catholic, while England was defiantly Protestant. England envied Spain's rich American colonies, while Spain resented English support for rebels in Spain's European lands. And both countries were led by proud, stubborn rulers.

Drake's voyage 1567-9
Drake's escape
Drake's voyage 1572-3

CARIBBEAN SEA

SOUTH AMERICA

FROM 1567-73, Francis Drake made many pirate raids on new Spanish settlements on the shores of the Caribbean Sea. He wanted to seize treasure and make himself rich.

IN 1572, while exploring in Panama, Drake caught his first glimpse of the Pacific Ocean. No English ship had sailed there as it was territory claimed by Spain.

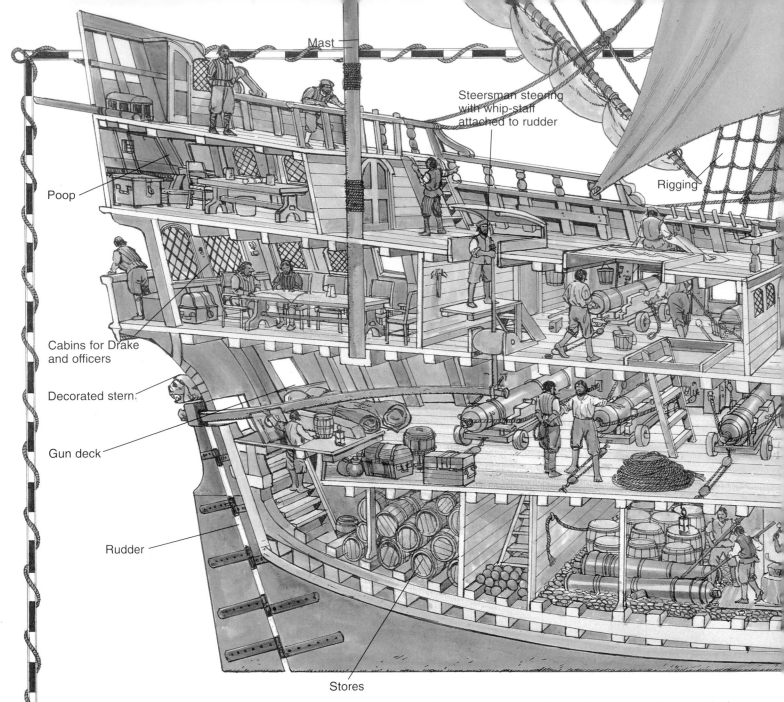

Mast

Steersman steering
with whip-staff
attached to rudder

Rigging

Poop

Cabins for Drake
and officers

Decorated stern

Gun deck

Rudder

Stores

A Secret Plan

Drake spent three years as a pirate, raiding ships and settlements all round the Spanish Main. It was an exciting way of life – risky, but profitable. At first, he was content to sail the Atlantic and Caribbean seas, but before long, he began to think of an ambitious new plan. He would sail into the Pacific Ocean – and maybe around the world – and attack Spanish possessions there.

Drake knew that Spanish treasure fleets sailed along the west coast of America, carrying gold, silver and emeralds from the mines of Peru, in South America. There were also many prosperous Spanish settlements along the Pacific Coast.

A voyage like this was bound be costly, so Drake had to find backers to help him buy a suitable ship. He asked Queen Elizabeth I of England, and several wealthy nobles. They agreed to give him the money he needed, in return for a share of any profits he made on the voyage.

Drake also had to invent a story to conceal his plan. At this time, in 1575, England and Spain were hostile to each other, but neither side wanted a war.

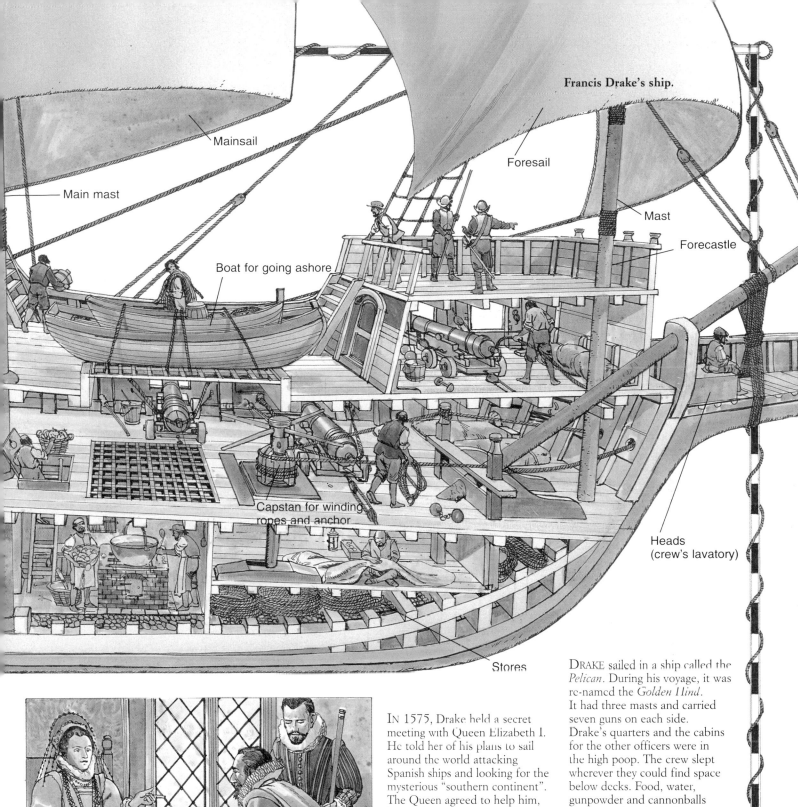

Francis Drake's ship.

Mainsail

Main mast

Foresail

Mast

Forecastle

Boat for going ashore

Capstan for winding ropes and anchor

Heads (crew's lavatory)

Stores

IN 1575, Drake held a secret meeting with Queen Elizabeth I. He told her of his plans to sail around the world attacking Spanish ships and looking for the mysterious "southern continent". The Queen agreed to help him, but said no one must ever know.

DRAKE sailed in a ship called the *Pelican*. During his voyage, it was re-named the *Golden Hind*. It had three masts and carried seven guns on each side. Drake's quarters and the cabins for the other officers were in the high poop. The crew slept wherever they could find space below decks. Food, water, gunpowder and cannonballs were stored in the hull.

Drake pretended to his noble backers that he would be seeking the mysterious "southern continent" that was supposed to lie somewhere below the equator. In AD 150, the geographer Ptolemy had suggested it was there. Magellan and del Cano had not found it on their voyage, but who knew how much more of the world was still to be discovered?

Troubles and Treasures

Drake set sail from the port of Plymouth, in south-west England, in December 1577. By Christmas, he had reached North Africa and had already captured two Spanish ships. He sailed on to the Cape Verde Islands to get fresh food and water. There, he seized a Portuguese trading ship and a Portuguese sea-pilot who had experience of sailing in the Pacific and around the South American coast.

It was April 1578 before he next saw land, in present-day Brazil. Like Magellan before him, Drake faced problems among his crew. The sailors were resentful – Drake had not told them he planned to sail around the world – and the officers quarreled among themselves. By late summer, these troubles were intolerable. There were fights, secret plots and even witchcraft on board. Drake executed the leading "wizard" and removed all privileges from the officers. Everyone was equally under his command.

Peace was restored, but then the weather seemed set against them. Three of Drake's five ships had already been lost in storms. The rest headed southwards, with difficulty, towards the Magellan Strait. When they finally entered the Pacific, they were blown far south of Tierra del Fuego (at the tip of South America) by terrifying gales. The *Marigold* sank, and the crew of the *Elizabeth* turned back for home. Only the *Golden Hind* survived to sail northwards as far as Canada, raiding and looting Spanish ships along the way.

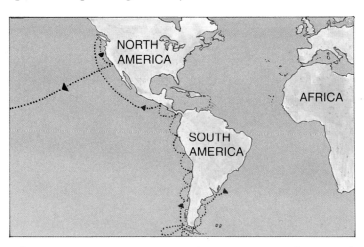

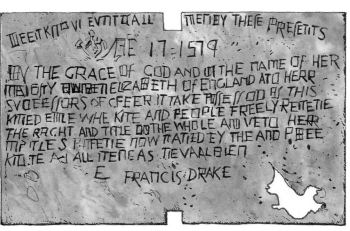

DRAKE'S ROUTE, April 1578-June 1579, round the American coast. Drake and his crew sailed into dangerous fog and a storm that lasted for a month. Only one of Drake's five ships survived.

BEFORE LEAVING New Albion (present-day California), Drake put up a metal plaque claiming the land for England and Queen Elizabeth. It is thought to still be there.

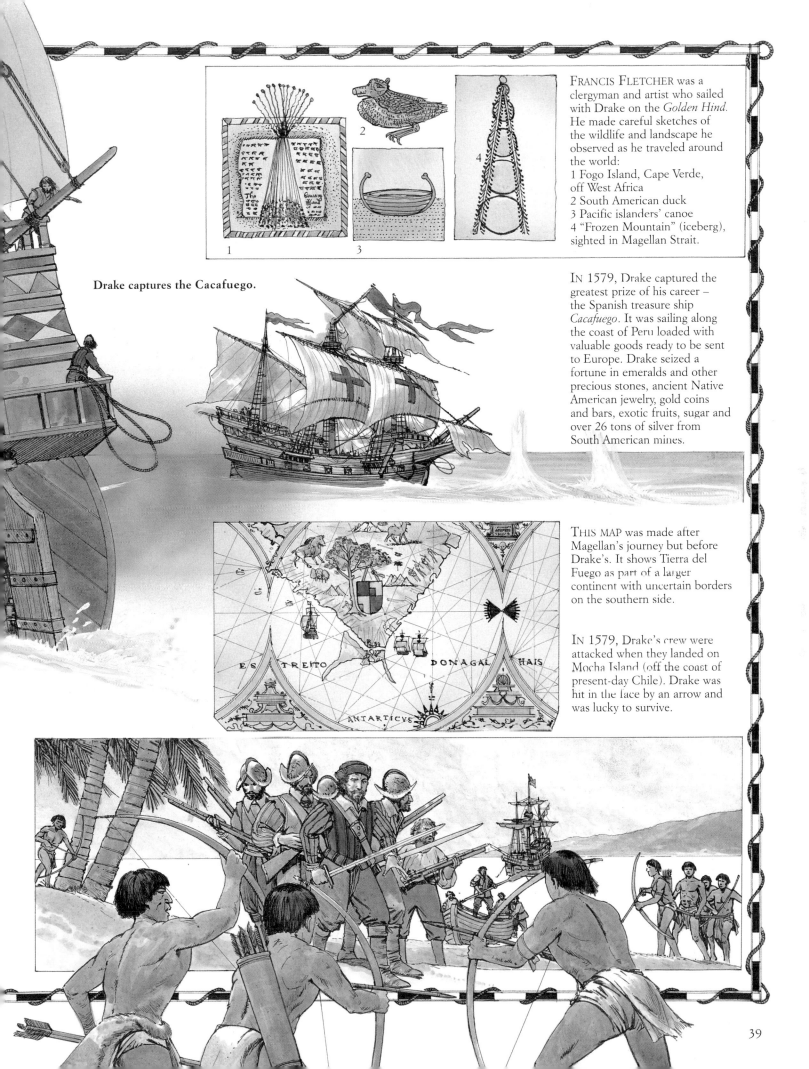

FRANCIS FLETCHER was a clergyman and artist who sailed with Drake on the *Golden Hind.* He made careful sketches of the wildlife and landscape he observed as he traveled around the world:
1 Fogo Island, Cape Verde, off West Africa
2 South American duck
3 Pacific islanders' canoe
4 "Frozen Mountain" (iceberg), sighted in Magellan Strait.

Drake captures the Cacafuego.

IN 1579, Drake captured the greatest prize of his career – the Spanish treasure ship *Cacafuego.* It was sailing along the coast of Peru loaded with valuable goods ready to be sent to Europe. Drake seized a fortune in emeralds and other precious stones, ancient Native American jewelry, gold coins and bars, exotic fruits, sugar and over 26 tons of silver from South American mines.

THIS MAP was made after Magellan's journey but before Drake's. It shows Tierra del Fuego as part of a larger continent with uncertain borders on the southern side.

IN 1579, Drake's crew were attacked when they landed on Mocha Island (off the coast of present-day Chile). Drake was hit in the face by an arrow and was lucky to survive.

Good Prospects for Trade

In midsummer, 1579, Drake left the Pacific coast of America, and steered a course westwards towards the Philippines. In September, the *Golden Hind* reached the remote island of Guam. Everyone on board looked forward to fresh food and water, but they had a disappointment in store. The local people threw stones at them and tried to sink their ship. Six weeks later, when Drake reached the Philippines, he was relieved to see friendly people waving from the shore. But the winds were too strong, and from the wrong direction, to allow him to land. He finally reached the Spice Islands in November 1579, after five exhausting months at sea.

Drake and his crew rested and repaired their ship. But Drake found time for business too. The local sultan was friendly and there were good prospects for trade. Drake met a Chinese merchant who invited him to visit him in Canton. Drake refused since he was already a very long way from home.

In early 1580, the *Golden Hind* set sail again, heading west towards the Indian Ocean and eventually, for home. A few days later, it hit a coral reef. This was the most dangerous moment in the voyage. The crew were scared they would be stuck there helplessly for ever, but the *Golden Hind* floated off at high tide, miraculously unharmed. By March 1580, they had reached Java, where they stopped to do more trading and be entertained by the local ruler. In June they sighted south Africa but hoped they would be home again soon.

MAP OF THE SPICE ISLANDS, drawn by a Dutch geographer around 1594. By then, 70 years after Magellan's voyage, European explorers had surveyed and recorded the coasts of many South-East Asian islands.

IN NOVEMBER 1569, the *Golden Hind* reached the island of Ternate, in the Spice Islands. The local sultan (king) was friendly and sailed out to inspect Drake and his ship.

DRAKE'S ROUTE September 1579-July 1580. By the time the *Golden Hind* landed in Sierra Leone (in north-west Africa), everyone on board was ill and desperately short of water.

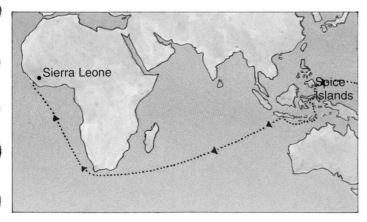

Sierra Leone

Spice Islands

ON THE ISLAND OF JAVA, Drake was entertained by royalty. The Sultan was fond of music and ordered the palace orchestra to perform to entertain his guests. Then he discussed business with Drake.

THEY AGREED on an exclusive deal, giving Drake and his backers – including Queen Elizabeth – the right to buy rare spices in the Sultan's lands.

Drake is met by the Sultan of Java.

Arise, Sir Francis

By June 22, 1580, Drake and his crew had reached north-west Africa. Conditions on the *Golden Hind* were grim, and 26 men had died. The survivors went ashore where they ate oysters and lemons: foods rich in vitamins that saved many sailors' lives.

On September 26, Drake reached his home port of Plymouth. He felt triumphant. He was only the second man to have sailed right around the world, and unlike Magellan and del Cano, he was bringing his ship home laden with treasure.

Drake felt anxious too. He had robbed many Spanish ships and sailors during his voyage. What would the Queen think about that? He had been away from home for three years. What if England had made peace with Spain? But Drake need not have worried. Queen Elizabeth was more concerned to discover how much treasure Drake had seized. She was delighted with the jewels he presented to her, and commanded him to bring the rest of his treasure to London. Then it could be shared out among everyone who had backed Drake's voyage – including herself. Drake's backers got a magnificent reward. For every pound they had invested, Drake was able to give them £4,700 profit in return.

The Queen allowed Drake to keep a rich fortune for himself, then told him to sail the *Golden Hind* round to Tilbury – a port on the River Thames. There, she went on board and made "her pirate" kneel before her. "Arise, Sir Francis Drake", she said.

DRAKE'S coat of arms, given to him by Queen Elizabeth when she made him a knight.

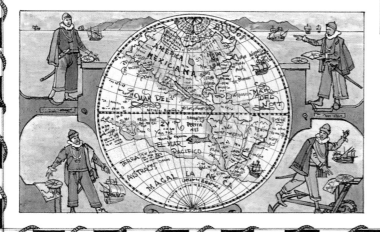

THIS SILVER CUP was given to Drake by Queen Elizabeth. It was made to hold the rare and precious coconut which Drake brought back from the Pacific and presented to the Queen.

DRAKE had not found the mysterious southern continent, but even after his return, maps were still made suggesting it was there. Eventually, Dutch explorer Abel Tasman sighted it in 1642.

Queen Elizabeth on board
the Golden Hind.

TWO EPIC VOYAGES

1480 MAGELLAN born to noble family in Portugal.

c. 1490 Del Cano born to ordinary family in Basque country (northern Spain).

1495 Magellan sent to fight in India.

1505 Magellan sent to fight in Spice Islands.

1511 Magellan returns to Europe, then to Morocco.

1517 Magellan asks King Manuel to sponsor voyage to seek westward route to Spice Islands. Manuel refuses, so Magellan seeks help from King Charles of Spain – Portugal's trading rival and old enemy.

1518 King of Spain agrees to back Magellan. King Manuel tries to sabotage Magellan's voyage.

1519 (August/September) Magellan sets sail with five ships and 237 men.

1519 (December) Crew mutinous.

1520 (March) Mutiny. Magellan hangs ringleaders. Del Cano is one of mutineers, but Magellan needs his navigational skills.

1520 (October/November) Discovers Magellan Strait. Sails through it to Pacific Ocean.

1521 (January) Sails past Pacific islands but cannot land. All on board sick and almost starving.

1521 (March) Arrive at Philippines; welcomed by local chief. They agree to help him fight.

1521 (April) Magellan killed in local war. Ships worn out and rotten.

Only about 115 crew alive. Go on pirate raids.

1521 (June) Leave Philippines for Spice Islands.

1521 (November) Arrive Spice Islands. Del Cano decides that *Vittoria* will sail west to Europe; *Trinidad* loaded with cloves, will sail back taking eastwards route. But *Trinidad* captured by Portuguese. Four men reach home.

1522 (March) *Vittoria* arrives off Mozambique (south-east Africa), which is occupied by Portuguese. Blown far south of Cape of Good Hope.

1522 (June) *Vittoria* sails across Equator. All on board are weak and ill.

1522 *Vittoria* lands Cape Verde Islands – chased by Portuguese; 13 crew imprisoned.

1522 (September) *Vittoria* reaches Seville. Del Cano a hero.

1522 (September) Sailors imprisoned on Cape Verde are freed. Del Cano and crew meet King Charles of Spain.

1525 Del Cano dies at sea, trying to make second round-the-world voyage.

MAGELLAN'S AND DRAKE'S epic voyages started a whole new era of long-distance trade and travel. In the centuries that followed, European ships and settlers made contact with different civilizations in many parts of the world.

1540/43 DRAKE born in Devon, south-west England.

1566 Drake's first voyage to Africa and the Caribbean, as slave trader with John Hawkins.

1568 Drake's ship attacked by Spanish at San Juan d'Ulloa, Mexico. Leads to lifelong hatred of Spain.

1572 Drake sails to Plymouth with five ships and 120 men.

1588 (January/February) To Cape Verde Islands. Crosses Atlantic (two months out of sight of land).

1588 (April-August) Arrives Argentina. Crew mutinous (Drake executes ringleader); weather foul.

Ships damaged in storm; only two survive.

1588 (August/September) Sails though Magellan Strait into Pacific. More storms; only one ship (*Golden Hind*) survives. Blown south – no sign of southern continent. Caribbean, as pirate. Raids Spanish settlements; sees Pacific.

1575 Drake plans round-the-world expedition to seek southern continent and attack Spanish ships and trading

posts in Spice Islands. Gets secret backing from Queen Elizabeth – English government and church leaders are hostile to Spain.

1577 (December) Leaves Plymouth with five ships and 120 men.

1588-9 (November-June) Explores west coast of America. Captures *Cacafuego*. Sails westwards.

1579 (October) Reaches Philippines but winds too strong to land. Sails on to Spice Islands.

1579 (November) Reaches Spice Islands; does spice-trading deal. Sails on.

1580 (January) *Golden Hind* almost wrecked on coral reef. Crew expect to die. But ship floats off reef in high tide.

1580 (March) Reaches Java. Entertained by Sultan of Java.

1580 (June) Sails past Cape of Good Hope (South Africa). Food and water finished.

1580 (July) Crew very ill. Lands Sierra Leone (north-west Africa) for oysters and fresh fruit.

1580 (September) Reaches Pymouth.

1581 (April) Sails *Golden Hind* to London; Queen Elizabeth comes on board and knights Drake.

1588 Drake plays leading part in fighting against invading Spanish Armada.

1596 Drake dies of fever on pirate voyage to Caribbean; buried at sea.

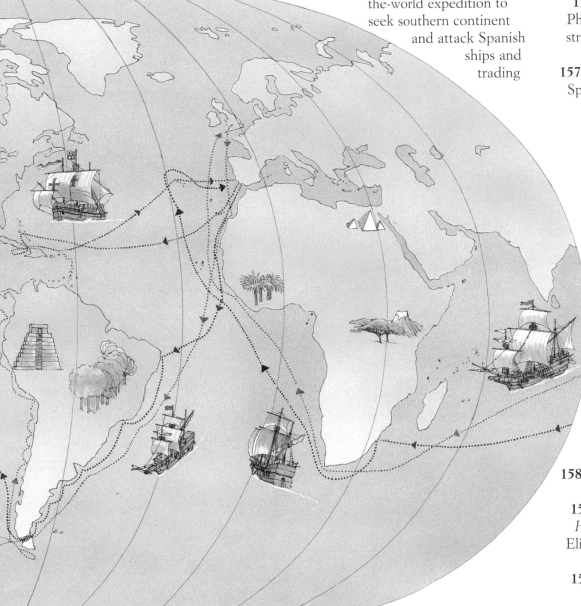

TIME CHART

VOYAGES EAST
(Voyages to Africa, India and the Far East by the eastward route)

1418   Prince Henry the Navigator sets up court at Sagres on the coast of Portugal. Begins to sponsor voyages of exploration to West Africa.

1439   Portuguese sailors reach the Azores.

1460   Henry the Navigator dies. Portuguese sailors reach Sierra Leone.

1469-75   Fernão Gomes (Portuguese) explores the west coast of Africa as far as present-day Angola.

1487-8   Bartolomeu Dias (Portuguese) sails round Cape of Good Hope. Enters Indian Ocean.

1487-99   Vasco da Gama (Portuguese) sails round Cape of Good Hope, across Indian Ocean and reaches Goa (on west coast of India).

1500   Gonzalo Cabral (Portuguese) sails across Atlantic and sights Brazil.

1509   First Portuguese voyage (round Cape of Good Hope) to Malacca (in present-day Malaysia).

1512-13   First Portuguese voyage (round Cape of Good Hope) to the Spice Islands (Moluccas).

1514   First Portuguese voyage (round Cape of Good Hope) to China (Canton).

VOYAGES NORTH
(Voyages aiming to reach the East by north-eastern and north-western routes)

1497   Cabot (English) sails to Newfoundland; thinks he has reached Asia.

1500   Corte-Real (Spanish) sails to Greenland.

1524   Verranzano (Italian) explores north-east coast of North America.

1534-5   Cartier (French) explores Saint Lawrence estuary (Canada).

1553   Willoughby and Chancellor (English) sail round North Cape (northern tip of Norway).

1574   Frobisher (English) sails to Baffin Island (nothern Canada); believes he has found strait leading to Pacific.

1587   Davis (English) explores Greenland.

1596-7   Barents (Dutch) sails to Bear Island, Spitzbergen and Novaya Zemlya (islands off Arctic Russia); his ships are trapped all winter by ice.

VOYAGES WEST
(Voyages aiming to reach the East by the westward route)

1492   Christopher Columbus (Italian, but with Spanish backing) sails across Atlantic and lands in the Bahamas, believes he has reached Japan.

1493-4   Columbus explores Cuba, believes it is China.

1498   Columbus reaches Trinidad and then Venezuela; believes he has arrived at mainland Asia.

1499-1500   Ojeda (Spanish) and Vespucci (Italian) cross the Atlantic, seeking Asia; they report the existence of River Amazon.

1502-4   Columbus explores Honduras, Nicaragua and Panama; believes he has reached Vietnam.

1519-22   Magellan (Portuguese, but with Spanish backing) and del Cano (Spanish) sail westwards in search of the Spice Islands. Magellan dies in the Philippines, but del Cano and some of Magellan's crew reach them eventually. They return home, still heading westwards. They make first-ever circumnavigation of the globe.

1525   Del Cano dies at sea while making second attempt at westwards voyage to the Spice Islands.

1527   Savedra (Spanish) pioneers sea-route from west coast of Mexico across the Pacific to the Spice Islands.

1565   Urdaneta (Spanish) discovers route across the Pacific from Philippines to Mexico avoiding easterly trade winds.

1577-80   Drake (English) hopes to capture Spanish trading posts in Spice Islands and to discover southern continent south of Magellan Strait; makes second circumnavigation of the globe.

GLOSSARY

Armillary sphere
a model showing stars and planets in the skies above the Earth. It helped sailors work out their position at sea by observing which stars were overhead.

Astrolabe
a metal disk with pointers used to measure the height of the Sun (or the Pole Star) above the horizon. Used by sailors to calculate their latitude and so work out their position at sea.

Astronomy
the study of the Sun, Moon, stars and planets.

Caravel
a small, light sailing ship with a triangular sail. It was fast and easy to steer.

Carrack
a ship with big square sails and a huge hull, designed to carry lots of cargo.

Caulking
a way of waterproofing ships' hulls by packing hemp fibres into cracks between the timbers.

Circumnavigation
a voyage around the earth.

Cross-staff
long wooden stick, fitted with cross-pieces called transoms. It helped sailors calculate their latitude and work out their position at sea.

Hemp
a plant with a long, tough stalk. Fibers from hemp stalks were twisted together to make rope.

Horizon
the "line" you see where the sky meets the land or the sea.

Hulk
an old rotting ship no longer able to make sea voyages.

Kemal
a square of animal horn fixed to a knotted rope, used by sailors to measure the angle of the Sun above the horizon and to calculate their latitude.

Latitude
position north or south of the equator.

Lead-line
heavy weights tied to long ropes, used to measure the depth of the sea.

Log-line
a knotted rope, trailed over the side of a moving ship, used to measure how fast it was traveling.

Navigation
the skill of sailing a ship.

Patriotic
loyal to your homeland.

Scurvy
a disease caused by lack of vitamin C.

Spanish Main
land and sea in and around the Caribbean, controlled by Spain in the 16th century.

Traverse board
wooden board used to record a ship's movements at sea.

INDEX